Short Stack Editions | Volume 18

# *Chocolate*

## by Susie Heller

**Short Stack Editions**

Publisher: Nick Fauchald
Creative Director: Rotem Raffe
Editor: Kaitlyn Goalen
Copy Editor: Abby Tannenbaum
Director of Development: Mackenzie Smith

ISBN 978-0-9907853-7-8

Printed in New York City
November 2015

# Table of Contents

# Desserts

# Drinks

***First things first:*** We have to give a hat tip to Susie Heller.

We were thrilled for the chance to collaborate with Susie, whose work on pivotal projects such as *The French Laundry Cookbook* has set the standard for the entire publishing industry.

But when she suggested chocolate for her edition, we raised our eyebrows—not because we don't love chocolate, but because so does pretty much everybody else in the world. Chocolate is an ingredient so universally adored that the idea of tackling it in a succinct cookbook seemed beyond challenging. How do you pay homage to all of the brilliant chocolate classics out there while still leaving room for exciting new inventions and discoveries? Well, we thought, if anyone is up to the task, it's Susie.

In the recipes that follow, Susie does a masterful job of visiting all the touchstones that chocolate lovers would expect to see (of all the chocolate cakes in the world, her confidently basic layer cake is the only recipe you'll ever need), in addition to catering to those seeking new ideas (cocoa nibs in a pepper mill, anyone?).

The result is satisfying on every level and sets a new bar for how chocolate can serve you in your cooking.

—*The Editors*

# Introduction

Surveys say that vanilla is America's most popular flavor. In my eyes, though, just the mention of chocolate dispels that myth. Whether it's in the form of an elaborate dessert or a tiny square nibbled from a bar, chocolate elicits smiles and feels like a luxury.

But it's a luxury that's also universal.

My first chocolate memory—of licking a chocolate-covered spatula at the kitchen counter—is such a frequently recalled childhood image that it's almost a rite of passage. The same is true of first chocolate bars. For me, it was a milk chocolate in the shape of an orange, with an almost neon-colored orange foil wrap, that an older cousin brought for me and my sister whenever she came to visit. I coveted it, rapping it on the table and watching it fall into sections. As I got older, I found my love of dark chocolate as I sipped my first drinking chocolate (the grown-up version of hot chocolate) at Angelina in Paris. I still consider it one of the most decadent treats.

My Hungarian mother loved to bake, and I'd wake up every morning to the smell of something coming from the oven. I started baking as a kid, when my choices were limited to Baker's unsweetened or semisweet chocolate, Hershey's milk chocolate or Nestlé's Toll House chocolate chips. Today, choosing chocolate is an art in itself. Chocolate, like wine or coffee, has subtle nuances in flavor, so picking one is all about tasting and finding the variety you like best.

There is much written about why we crave chocolate and the science behind it. For me, it's about flavor and texture. Break off a piece of chocolate and listen for the snap, smell its subtle aroma, place it in your mouth and let it melt slowly and fill your mouth with its unique flavor.

Although I love to eat chocolate out of hand, I'm even more enamored with it as a source of inspiration in recipes. Chocolate is a staple in my pantry. I constantly experiment with it in both desserts and other dishes. My refrigerator usually contains some kind of homemade chocolate sauce, just bits of leftover chocolates, melted and thinned with some cream. Warm chocolate sauce poured over ice cream always seems perfect. I use a rasp grater to grate dark chocolate into soft goat cheese with a bit of honey for an easy appetizer. And then there is another favorite childhood memory: When I was sick, my mother grated chocolate over a hot bowl of cream of wheat. I always felt better.

In this volume, I've included a wide range of my favorite chocolate recipes. Most of them are sweet, of course, but I've added a couple of savory applications as well. Some are very simple, some are more elaborate, some lighter, some richer, but all are recipes I rely on to showcase a universally loved ingredient.

Enjoy!

—*Susie Heller*

# Recipes

# Chocolate Gingerbread

One of my favorite desserts is moist gingerbread. I'm not a fan of ground ginger, so my version uses fresh ginger—specifically ginger juice, which prevents small pieces of fresh ginger from interfering with the lovely texture of the gingerbread. Chocolate works beautifully with the classic roster of gingerbread spices, adding an extra layer of depth and earthiness. Serve squares of gingerbread alone or topped with lightly whipped cream.

8 tablespoons (1 stick) unsalted butter, at room temperature, plus more for the pan

One 4-ounce piece of fresh ginger, peeled

1 cup mild molasses

1 teaspoon baking soda

2½ cups all-purpose flour

1 tablespoon baking powder

1 teaspoon ground cinnamon

1 teaspoon kosher salt

Pinch of ground cloves

1 cup firmly packed light brown sugar

1 large egg

½ teaspoon pure vanilla extract

5 ounces 66% semisweet chocolate, melted, at room temperature

Lightly sweetened whipped cream (optional)

**serves 12**

Preheat the oven to 350°. Butter a 9-by-13-by-2-inch baking pan.

Finely grate the ginger, preferably on a Microplane, over a bowl. Place a fine-mesh strainer over another bowl and transfer the ginger to the strainer. Press on the ginger to extract all the juice. Discard the pulp. You should have about 2 tablespoons of ginger juice.

Bring 1½ cups of water to a boil in a small saucepan. Remove from the heat and stir in the molasses and baking soda. Cool for about 15 minutes while you make the gingerbread.

In a small bowl, whisk together the flour, baking powder, cinnamon, salt and cloves. In the bowl of a stand mixer fitted with the paddle attachment, beat the butter and sugar at medium-high speed until light and fluffy, about 3 minutes. Scrape down the side of the bowl and beat in the egg and vanilla to combine. With the mixer at low speed, alternately add one-third of the dry ingredients, followed by one-third of the molasses mixture, allowing each addition to be completely incorporated before adding the rest in thirds. Scrape down the side of the bowl as necessary.

Mix in the melted chocolate and remove the mixer from the stand. Using a silicone spatula, scrape the bottom of the bowl to be certain that all the ingredients are incorporated in the batter.

Pour the batter into the prepared pan and bake for 35 minutes or until a skewer inserted into the center comes out clean. Cool the gingerbread in the pan before cutting into pieces. Serve with whipped cream, if desired.

## Melting Chocolate

Years ago, I tried melting chocolate in a microwave and it was a disaster—it turns out that even chocolate can be nasty if you burn it to a crisp. As a result, I returned to the tried-and-true method of melting it in a double boiler. I recommend the following technique: Melt about three quarters of the chocolate over medium heat (a double boiler will make it extra easy), then remove it from the heat and stir in the remaining chocolate. Doing so will help cool it down enough to handle easily.

With trepidation, I've revisited the microwave method, and the key to success here is constant vigilance. Heat the chocolate for 20 to 30 seconds, give it a good stir, then continue to heat the chocolate in 10-second intervals until it's melted. I usually remove it from the microwave when about three-quarters of the chocolate has melted, and then stir until all the chocolate has melted.

# Almond-Cocoa Nib Shortbread Cookies

Shortbread cookies are crisp, sugary and perfect with a cup of tea or coffee. I've added brown rice flour and almond meal to this traditional cookie, which cuts down on the gluten in the recipe while adding a nutty flavor. Adding chopped cocoa nibs and chocolate on the top of the dough makes the cookies look like the spots of a Dalmatian (my husband's favorite breed of dog). Who says you can't improve on a classic?

1 cup all-purpose flour

¼ cup plus 2 tablespoons brown rice flour

¼ cup plus 2 tablespoons almond meal

12 tablespoons (1½ sticks) unsalted butter, at room temperature

½ cup sugar

½ teaspoon pure vanilla extract

Pinch of kosher salt

1 tablespoon finely chopped cocoa nibs

2 tablespoons finely chopped semisweet or bittersweet chocolate

makes ·24·

Position the oven racks in the lower and upper thirds of the oven and preheat the oven to 325°. Line two baking sheets with parchment paper.

In a bowl, combine the all-purpose flour, brown rice flour and almond meal.

In the bowl of a stand mixer fitted with the paddle attachment, beat the butter and sugar at medium-low speed for about 2 minutes, scraping down the bowl as necessary. Mix in the vanilla. Add the salt and flour mixture. Beat until the mixture is thoroughly combined and beginning to hold together.

Transfer the dough to a work surface and press it together using the heel of your hand. Place the dough on a piece of parchment paper. Top with another piece of parchment and roll to ¼-inch thickness. Remove the top piece of parchment, sprinkle the surface of the dough with the nibs and chocolate, then top again with parchment and roll gently to press the nibs and chopped chocolate into the dough. Move the dough (still between the pieces of parchment) to a baking sheet and refrigerate for at least 30 minutes to harden.

Using a 2-inch-round cookie cutter or drinking glass, cut rounds from the dough and arrange them on the prepared baking sheets, leaving at least 1 inch between the cookies. Trimmings can be gently pushed back together, rerolled and cut into more rounds.

Bake for 20 to 24 minutes, reversing the position of the baking sheets from top to bottom and from front to back after 10 minutes, until the cookies are golden brown.

Place the sheets on cooling racks and cool the shortbread for about 3 minutes to firm up a bit, then transfer the cookies to the racks to cool completely. Store in an airtight container.

# Chocolate Pancakes

This rich breakfast is a variation on the chocolate-chip pancakes you were so keen on as a kid. By adding almonds, coconut and honey, I've rendered them suitable for all ages. Because flour is replaced with almond meal, I fold in egg whites to make the pancakes lighter. In addition to being delicious, the pancakes are gluten-free. Serving them with Chocolate Butter reinforces the chocolate flavor, but use a high-quality maple syrup if you prefer.

½ cup almond meal

2 tablespoons shredded unsweetened coconut

1 ounce 72% to 82% chocolate, grated

¼ teaspoon kosher salt

2 large eggs

¼ cup heavy cream

½ teaspoon pure vanilla extract

1 tablespoon honey

Coconut oil

Chocolate Butter (optional; see recipe on page 15)

Maple syrup (optional)

*makes*
**-12-**

In a medium mixing bowl, stir together the almond meal, coconut, chocolate and salt. Separate the eggs, placing the yolks in a small bowl and the whites in a metal mixing bowl. Add the cream, vanilla and honey to the bowl with the yolks and beat with a fork. Stir the yolk mixture into the dry ingredients until combined.

Whisk the egg whites until soft peaks begin to form. Stir about one quarter of the whites into the batter, then fold in the remaining whites. Heat a film of coconut oil in a large nonstick skillet or griddle over medium-low heat. When the oil is hot, spoon 2 tablespoons of batter into the skillet. Using a small offset spatula, spread it into a 3½-inch circle. Repeat with additional batter, taking care not to crowd the pan. These pancakes need to cook more gently than traditional pancakes.

There should be some bubbling of the coconut oil around the pancakes, but if they're browning too quickly, lower the heat. Cook until the bottom is set and lightly browned, 1 to 1½ minutes. Flip the pancakes and brown on the second side. Serve the pancakes immediately with of a pat of chocolate butter and/or warm maple syrup.

# *Chocolate Butter*

---

During Jacques Pépin's childhood, he ate baguettes with a piece of chocolate in them as a snack. I tried it and although I loved the combination of bread and chocolate, I missed the butter. This recipe bridges both components together for the best of both worlds. Flag it for using up any chocolate scraps you might have (rarely a problem in my house); feel free to use different types of chocolate here. Spread the butter on toast, muffins, scones, pancakes or crêpes. Whisk it into oatmeal or just use your imagination!

---

6 tablespoons (¾ stick) unsalted butter, at room temperature

2 ounces sweet chocolate, melted and cooled

½ teaspoon pure vanilla extract

Powdered sugar (optional)

Finely ground nuts or sea salt (optional)

In a stand mixer fitted with the paddle attachment, beat the butter and vanilla at medium speed until smooth and creamy. Beat in the chocolate. If you want to sweeten the butter, add powdered sugar. Fold in the nuts or sea salt to taste, if desired. Spoon the butter into a container or crock or roll it into a log.

To shape into a log, spoon the butter onto a 12-by-12-inch piece of plastic wrap in a rough log shape. Roll up the butter, twisting the ends of the plastic wrap to make the roll more compact. Tie the ends. To keep the log from sagging as it cools, drop the package into a bowl of ice water to harden, then remove it, pat dry and refrigerate.

# Nibby Strawberries

I have a bed of strawberries in my garden, and this simple dish has become one of my favorite ways to get through my harvest during strawberry season. It's not a chocolate dessert per se, but the freshly ground cocoa nibs add a hint-plus of chocolate flavor. Use sweet, juicy strawberries and the best balsamic vinegar you have. Topped with whipped cream, this becomes a surprisingly easy dessert (or morning-time sweet) in just a few minutes.

Fill a small, clean peppermill with **cocoa nibs**. (If you don't have a peppermill to repurpose for this, you can coarsely grind the nibs using a mortar and pestle or spice grinder.) Stem some **strawberries** and cut them vertically into 4 pieces.

In a bowl, combine about 2 parts **aged balsamic vinegar** with 1 part **superfine sugar** and stir to dissolve the sugar (for each cup of sliced berries, that would be 1 tablespoon vinegar to 1½ teaspoons sugar). Add a pinch of **salt**. Put the berries in a larger bowl and toss with the balsamic mixture to coat. Let the berries macerate for about 30 minutes.

Spoon the berries into serving bowls, adding a little of the macerating liquid. Spoon a dollop of **sweetened whipped cream** over the top. Pass the peppermill at the table to grind the cocoa nibs generously over the berries.

# Grilled Chicken Wings with Cocoa-Nib Rub & Honey Glaze

Chicken wings are a staple when I entertain, and I've experimented with dozens of dry rubs over the years. What I've found is that I prefer a simple rub. Here, the cocoa nibs add a rich flavor and nice contrast to the salt and pepper. When you add just the right amount of char from the grill and a light coating of honey, it's absolute perfection.

2 teaspoons kosher salt

2 teaspoons freshly ground black pepper

2 teaspoons cocoa nibs

1½ pounds whole chicken wings, at room temperature

Olive oil

Honey

**Serves 4 to 6**

Prepare a medium-hot gas or charcoal grill.

Pulse the salt, pepper and cocoa nibs in a spice grinder (or grind with a mortar and pestle) until the nibs are the texture of coarsely ground black pepper.

Leave the wings whole, or cut into thirds at the joints and discard the wing tips. Put the wings in a bowl and rub with a light coating of oil. Toss the wings with the rub to coat evenly.

Arrange the wings on the grill and cook, turning often, until cooked through, about 12 to 15 minutes. Remove from the grill and brush lightly with honey. Serve immediately.

# Chicken Cacahuate

Ask someone to name savory recipes made with chocolate, and Mexican mole is likely to be their first (and only) answer. But mole is also famously complicated to make from scratch. So I've turned to this recipe, which feawtures a distant cousin to mole that gets its richness from peanuts. I use white meat chicken for this dish, since that's how I was taught, but feel free to substitute dark meat if you prefer. And let this be just the beginning of your savory chocolate adventures. Try adding one ounce or so of unsweetened or bittersweet chocolate to dishes that have a combination of tomatoes and peppers—like chili, baked beans or barbecue sauce. It's that secret ingredient that can elevate the final product.

Canola oil

1 cup sliced yellow onion

2 whole garlic cloves

1¼ cups roasted peanuts, plus ⅓ cup coarsely chopped roasted peanuts, for garnish

¼ teaspoon ground cinnamon

¼ teaspoon freshly ground black pepper, plus more for seasoning

⅛ teaspoon ground cloves

One 28-ounce can whole peeled tomatoes with their juices

2 to 3 chipotle peppers in adobo sauce

3 cups chicken stock, divided

6 boneless skinless chicken breasts, at cool room temperature

Kosher salt

1½ ounces unsweetened chocolate, chopped

2 tablespoons cider vinegar

⅓ cup sliced scallions, for garnish

¼ cup cilantro leaves, for garnish

6 large lime wedges, for garnish

4 cups cooked rice, for serving

serves
-6-

Heat a thin film of canola oil in a large skillet over medium-high heat. Add the onion, lower the heat to medium and cook until the onion has softened and turned golden brown, about 7 minutes. Add the garlic and cook for another minute or two. Stirring constantly, add the whole peanuts, cinnamon, black pepper and cloves and cook until the spices are fragrant, about 1 minute.

Add the tomatoes and their juices, the chipotle peppers and any sauce that clings to them (2 peppers will make a medium-spicy sauce; three will make it very spicy) and 2 cups of the chicken stock. Bring to a simmer, cover, turn off the heat and let rest for at least 30 minutes.

Meanwhile, season both the chicken all over with salt and pepper Pour a film of canola oil in a second large skillet and heat over medium-high heat. Add the chicken and brown on both sides, about 5 minutes. Remove from the pan.

Transfer the tomato mixture to a food processor or blender and puree until completely smooth. Strain (pressing on any solids) through a strainer into a large saucepan. Bring to a simmer. Stir in the chocolate until it's melted. Add the vinegar and submerge the chicken in the sauce. If the sauce doesn't cover the chicken or seems too thick, stir in some or all of the remaining 1 cup of chicken stock. Simmer, partially covered, for 25 minutes or until the chicken is cooked through.

Serve the chicken, either whole or sliced, with a ladleful of sauce, and sprinkle each portion with a generous amount of the chopped peanuts, scallions and cilantro. Garnish each plate with a wedge of lime and pass a bowl of rice at the table.

# Chocolate Pasta

Incorporating cocoa into fresh pasta enhances it with a beautiful rich-brown color and subtle cocoa flavor. I serve these fresh noodles with tomato-based sauces such as Bolognese or marinara. To take this recipe over the top, add 1 ounce of chopped bittersweet chocolate to your sauce while it simmers. That small amount of chocolate makes a huge difference in the sauce's flavor, and will only amplify the richness in the chocolate pasta. This is a very delicate pasta, so cook it just before serving.

1 cup semolina flour, plus more for dusting the pasta

1 cup all-purpose flour, plus more for dusting the dough

⅓ cup unsweetened cocoa powder

2 teaspoons walnut or olive oil

About ¾ cup lukewarm water, divided

serves
4 to 6

Put the flours in the bowl of a stand mixer fitted with the dough hook. Sift in the cocoa. Turn the machine to low speed and add the oil. Pour in ½ cup of the water; once the ingredients are moistened, turn the mixer to medium speed. Continue to add small amounts of water, scraping the bowl as necessary, until the dough begins to come together around the hook. Stop the machine and turn the dough over in the bowl, pressing to pick up any stray pieces, particularly in the bottom of the bowl.

Mix at medium speed to knead the dough for 8 more minutes. Check the dough; it should be smooth and soft. If it's sticky, beat in small amounts of additional semolina flour.

Remove the dough from the mixer and knead a few times by hand to bring the dough together into a smooth mass. Shape into a 1-inch-thick square and wrap in plastic wrap. Let the dough rest at room temperature for at least 30 minutes or refrigerate for up to 2 days. It's best to roll the dough and cut the pasta shortly before cooking it.

Cut the dough into 4 pieces and flatten each piece to about ¼-inch thickness. Dust both sides lightly with all-purpose flour. Roll through a pasta machine following the machine's instructions. If the dough sticks at all, dust with more flour as necessary. Cut into fettuccine or another shape you like. Toss lightly with semolina flour to prevent the pasta from sticking together.

Bring a large pot of salted water to a boil. When you're ready to serve the pasta, boil it in salted water for about 2 minutes or until cooked through. Drain and serve immediately with pasta sauce.

# Chocolate Peanut Popcorn Balls

A trip to Euclid Beach Amusement Park in Cleveland was one of my favorite summer activities growing up. I'm not sure what I liked more, the rides or the popcorn balls. These messy treats consisted of popcorn held together with a sticky-sweet syrup; despite having a mouth full of metal, I couldn't get enough. It's tough to improve on a childhood favorite, but adding chocolate and peanuts seems to do the trick. These popcorn balls are very chewy and chocolaty—and so easy to pack for a picnic.

Tip: Look for mushroom popcorn. It has extra-large kernels when it's popped, making it perfect for these balls.

Canola (or other mild oil), for coating utensils and your hands

8 cups unsalted popped popcorn (preferably mushroom popcorn)

1 cup sugar

⅓ cup light corn syrup

2 tablespoons unsweetened cocoa powder

1 teaspoon kosher salt

⅔ cup roasted, salted peanuts

makes 6

Preheat the oven to 300°. Line a baking sheet with parchment paper. Lightly oil the widest, largest metal bowl you have and put the popcorn in it. Lightly oil 2 silicone spatulas. If you have disposable plastic gloves, grab a pair, or pour some oil in a wide bowl to coat your hands with.

When you are ready to begin the syrup, put the bowl of popcorn in the oven.

In a medium saucepan, stir together the sugar, ½ cup of water, the corn syrup, cocoa and salt. Bring to a boil, stirring constantly, and cook until the mixture registers 250° on a candy thermometer. Carefully, because it will be hot, remove the bowl of popcorn from the oven and continue to cook the syrup to 255°. Depending on the size of your pot, this could take 15 to 20 minutes.

Immediately pour the syrup in the center of the popcorn and use the spatulas to toss the popcorn with the syrup. After a few tosses, add the peanuts and continue to toss and coat the popcorn. I like it when most of the kernels are coated but there is still some white visible.

As soon as you are able to handle the popcorn (it should still be warm), put on the gloves or coat your hands with a bit of oil and form the popcorn mixture into six 3-inch balls. Place the balls on the parchment. If the mixture hardens and becomes difficult to work with, return it to the oven to soften. When the balls are room temperature, wrap them individually in plastic wrap and store in an airtight container for up to 2 days (after that they will become excessively chewy).

# *Chocolate Meringue Straws*

---

Ever since I began cooking professionally, I've made meringues. First it was the classic meringue clouds that were painstaking to create. After years of crafting complicated desserts, I realized it was just as satisfying to make a more mellowed out version: meringue straws. Cocoa adds just the right touch to balance the richness of the sugar. I like to change things up by adding a variety of toppings.

Keep in mind that meringues do require slow drying in the oven. It's best to make them on a day that isn't humid. These can be served as part of a cookie plate, crushed over ice cream or on their own with a demitasse of Drinking Chocolate (page 42).

---

¾ cup superfine sugar

1 tablespoon unsweetened cocoa powder

3 large egg whites

¼ teaspoon salt

**makes 36**

¼ teaspoon pure vanilla extract

Chopped cocoa nibs, chopped pistachios, shredded coconut, crushed peppermint candy (optional)

Position the oven racks in the lower and upper thirds of the oven and preheat the oven to 200°. Place the sugar in a small bowl and sift in the cocoa. Stir to combine.

Line two baking sheets with parchment paper (baking sheets without rims work best). Using a ruler and a black marker, draw 5-inch-long lines that are 1½ inches apart on the paper to serve as a guide. Turn the parchment paper over; you'll still be able to see the lines.

In the bowl of a stand mixer fitted with the whisk attachment, beat the egg whites and salt at medium-high speed until the whites hold soft peaks. With the mixer running, gradually add the sugar mixture and vanilla. Increase the speed to high and whip for 3 to 4 minutes, until the meringue is thickened and glossy (when you lift some on the whisk, it will fall over gently). Transfer the meringue to a pastry bag fitted with a ⅜-inch tip.

Hold the pastry bag about ½ inch over the baking sheet and pipe straight lines following the guide. Sprinkle the sticks with a variety of toppings, such as chopped cocoa nibs, chopped pistachios, shredded coconut and crushed peppermint candy.

Bake for 3 to 3½ hours, rotating the pans from top to bottom and from front to back after 1½ hours, until the meringues are crisp and an edge releases from the parchment. At this point, the entire meringue will not release. Turn off the oven and leave the meringues inside for an hour. Gently run a palette knife or thin metal spatula under the meringues to loosen them from the parchment paper. Store in an airtight container at room temperature for several days or up to 2 weeks. The meringues will soften if they are exposed to damp air.

# Mascarpone-Filled Figs with Chocolate

I have a big fig tree in my backyard and have found that figs and chocolate make great partners. The addition of rich, creamy mascarpone seems to take that partnership to another level. Somewhere between sweet and savory, these figs make an excellent addition to a cheese course or dessert plate. They're best served within a few hours of making them.

Fresh figs

Mascarpone cheese, at room temperature (about 1 tablespoon per fig)

Honey (optional)

Tempered chocolate (see page 26)

Line a tray large enough to hold the figs with a piece of parchment paper. Wipe the figs, but avoid washing them. Check to be sure the figs will stand upright. If necessary, cut a small swatch from the bottom of the fig so it sits on a flat surface. Using a small spoon or melon baller, scoop out the center of the figs from the bottom to form a cavity.

If your figs are very sweet, there's no need to sweeten the mascarpone. Otherwise, whisk some honey into the mascarpone before filling the figs, tasting as you go to determine your preferred level of sweetness.

Fit a pastry bag with a plain tip, and fill the bag with mascarpone. You need about 1 tablespoon of mascarpone per fig. (You can also the mascarpone in a small heavy-duty plastic bag and cut off one corner to make a small opening.) Fill the cavity of the each fig with the mascarpone.

Holding them by the stems, dip the figs into the tempered chocolate, coating them about halfway up the sides. Stand the figs on the parchment paper and let sit at room temperature to allow the chocolate to harden before serving. It may take 2 to 3 hours, depending on the temperature of the room. (On a hot day, the figs can be refrigerated briefly to harden the chocolate.)

# Tempering Chocolate

Tempered chocolate is the key that locks so many chocolate-dipped combos. If you've never tempered before, it's exactly what it sounds like: Raising and lowering the temperature of melted chocolate changes its structure changes so that the chocolate will harden into a glossy coating. Unfortunately, I haven't really found a tempering method that's both easy and foolproof. But if you're willing to commit to the process, it produces plenty of worthwhile results.

Here's my method: Use chopped chocolate and have a reliable instant-read thermometer ready. Reserve one quarter of the chocolate you're tempering and put the remaining chocolate in the top of a double boiler set over an inch of simmering water.

When the chocolate has melted to 118° (dark chocolate) or 112° (milk chocolate), remove the top of the double boiler from the water and stir in the reserved quarter of chocolate. Stir constantly until the chocolate cools to 90° (dark chocolate) or 88° (milk chocolate). If the chocolate cools below the designated temperature, reheat it slowly over warm water to maintain the proper temperature.

The chocolate is now ready for dipping. To obtain the best coating, be sure that any ingredient you dip is dry before you dip it. Any liquid will cause the chocolate to seize. Check the temperature of the chocolate from time to time, reheating as necessary. Once you've dipped the ingredient, place it on a piece of parchment paper to set at room temperature. If the room is too hot to set in 2 to 3 hours, the dipped pieces can be refrigerated briefly to set.

# Chocolate Wine Biscuits

In Italy, you'll find crunchy ring-shaped wine biscuits served with cheese and a glass of wine. My nontraditional addition of cocoa powder results in a darker biscuit with a hit of toasted cocoa flavor. Black pepper adds extra depth, but you can eliminate it or add another spice, such as fennel seeds. If you like heat, add a pinch of cayenne pepper. I prefer baking these one batch at a time for the best results. I usually serve the biscuits at the end of the meal with three different cheeses, ranging in flavor (mild to assertive) and texture (creamy to hard). However, I've also been known to have a biscuit in the morning with a cup of coffee.

½ cup dry red wine

½ cup olive oil

1½ cups all-purpose flour, plus more if necessary

½ cup unsweetened cocoa powder

2 teaspoons baking powder

½ cup sugar, plus more for dusting

¼ teaspoon kosher salt

½ to 1 teaspoon freshly ground black pepper (optional)

Egg wash

*makes* **30**

Preheat the oven to 375°. Line two baking sheets with parchment paper.

Combine the wine and oil in a small bowl. In a large bowl, sift together the flour, cocoa and baking powder. Whisk in the sugar, salt and pepper. Add the wine and oil mixture to the flour mixture and use your fingers to mix the dough until the ingredients are well combined. Transfer to a floured work surface and knead until smooth. The mixture will be very shiny and soft, but if it is too soft to work with, you can add 1 tablespoon of additional flour at a time, just enough to be able to roll the dough.

Using your hands, roll 1 tablespoon of the dough into a rope that's about 5 inches long. Form the dough into a ring and overlap the ends to seal. Repeat with the remaining dough—you should have about 30 rings—and arrange the biscuits on the baking sheets, leaving space between them.

Bake the biscuits, one sheet at a time, for 10 minutes. Rotate the baking sheet from front to back and continue to bake for another 10 to 13 minutes. It's difficult to see when the biscuits are done because of their dark color, so don't be shy about breaking one open: The interior should be cooked throughout, while the exterior should have a nice crispness (it will continue to crisp up as it cools). Place the baking sheet on a cooling rack to cool for about 3 minutes (to let the biscuits firm up a bit), then transfer the biscuits to the rack to cool completely. Store in an airtight container for up to 1 week.

## Storing Chocolate

Keep your chocolate in an airtight container in a cool pantry. Milk chocolate is best if used within a year, while darker chocolates will be at their best for two years if they're stored properly. You may notice a white bloom on the chocolate; that discoloration is caused by the cocoa butter separating from the cocoa solids. The chocolate is still good, but I tend to use it in recipes calling for melted chocolate.

# Cocoa-Chai Ice Pops

I'd never had a cup of hot chai until a year ago. I'm really not sure why, since I love the flavor of the spices and I'm a huge fan of ginger. From the first sip, I knew I wanted to try chai in frozen form, and these popsicles are the result. The intensity of black tea, cocoa and the unexpected flavors of the spices translate beautifully to a dessert. You can adjust the amount of tea if you prefer a milder flavor. If you would like creamy pops, add the heavy cream. I like to freeze the chai in molds, but you can also add milk and pour it over ice for an iced chocolate-chai drink.

¼ cup unsweetened cocoa powder

½ cup turbinado sugar

Once 3-inch cinnamon stick

5 black peppercorns

Two thinly sliced 2-inch pieces of fresh ginger

6 green cardamom pods, cracked

2 cloves

1 star anise

Pinch of kosher salt

3 tablespoons loose black tea or 4 bags of black tea

½ cup heavy cream (optional)

*makes* **6**

Put the cocoa in a medium saucepan and measure out 2¼ cups of water. Whisk in enough of the water to make a paste, then add the remaining water and the sugar. Stir in the cinnamon, peppercorns, ginger, cardamom, cloves, star anise and salt. Bring to a boil, then remove from the heat, cover and let sit at room temperature for 15 minutes to infuse the flavors.

Return the liquid to a boil. Stir in the tea, remove from the heat, then cover the pan and let sit at room temperature for 5 minutes to infuse the flavors. Strain the liquid through a fine-mesh strainer and discard the solids. Stir in the heavy cream, if using. Pour the mixture into ice pop molds and freeze until solid.

# *The Best Chocolate Layer Cake*

This is my all-time favorite chocolate layer cake. I could never write a book on this ingredient without including it. It's rich chocolate all the way, the cake you dream about pairing with a big glass of cold milk (whole milk, please!): no nuts, no fancy embellishments. It's the one you remember under the glass dome at the diner. Kids and adults alike will love it. Bookmark this page and keep it close.

One thing to remember before you dive in: Be patient with allowing the frosting to cool at room temperature. You won't believe the shine!

---

*For the frosting:*

1¼ cups sugar

1 cup heavy cream

5 ounces unsweetened chocolate, finely chopped

8 tablespoons (1 stick) unsalted butter, cut into ½-inch pieces

1 teaspoon pure vanilla extract

*For the cake:*

Unsalted butter and flour, for the pan

2 cups sugar

1¾ cups all-purpose flour

¾ cup unsweetened cocoa powder, sifted

1 teaspoon kosher salt

1½ teaspoons baking powder

1½ teaspoons baking soda

2 large eggs, lightly beaten

½ cup canola oil

1 cup whole milk

1 cup boiling water

makes 8 to 10

Make the frosting (it's best to prepare the frosting a few hours before you plan to frost the cake): In a small saucepan, combine the sugar and cream. Bring to a boil over medium heat, stirring occasionally. Lower the heat and simmer for 6 minutes. Add the chocolate and butter and stir until melted. Pour into a bowl and stir in the vanilla. Let sit at room temperature until ready to use, whisking from time to time (don't over-whip the frosting or you'll create air bubbles).

Meanwhile, make the cake: Preheat the oven to 350°. Butter two 9-inch round cake pans. Line the bottoms with parchment paper, then butter and flour the top of the parchment and the sides of the pans.

In the bowl of a stand mixer fitted with the paddle attachment, combine the sugar, flour, cocoa, salt, baking powder and baking soda and beat at low speed. Mix in the eggs, oil and milk. Increase the speed to medium and beat for 2 minutes. Reduce the speed to low and mix in the water; the batter will be very loose. Remove the bowl from the mixer and scrape down the bottom and sides of the bowl with a spatula.

Divide the batter between the cake pans and bake for 30 to 35 minutes, or until a cake tester or toothpick inserted in the center comes out clean. Transfer to a cooling rack, let cool for 5 minutes, then turn the layers out onto the rack and let cool completely.

Check the frosting. It should have the consistency of mayonnaise. If it's too loose, let it cool longer, stirring occasionally.

Place the bottom layer of the cake on a plate. Spread about ¾ cup of the frosting over the bottom layer. Top with the second layer. Spread the remaining frosting over the top and, if desired, sides of the cake. For a glossier finish, run a palette knife under hot water, dry completely with a towel, and then run the hot knife over the frosting. This cake is best eaten the day it is made, but leftovers can be covered and refrigerated.

# Chocolate-Ricotta Fritters with Peaches & Honey

I love doughnuts (who doesn't?), but most recipes yield heavy, over-the-top versions that require a nap after eating. Thanks to the addition of ricotta, these fritters are light and delicate, and their soft insides make an excellent vehicle for the flavor of the chocolate to shine through. In the summer, I always serve the fritters with ripe fruit at the peak of flavor. Fruit marinated in honey and a sweet wine provide the perfect contrast to the hot fritters. The fritter batter can be made and held for several hours before frying, which makes serving them as dessert for guests easy. Be ready to prepare and assemble the fritters so that you can eat them while they're hot and crisp.

**For the peaches:**

¼ cup honey

¼ cup Sauternes or sweet Riesling wine

1 cup (about 2 medium) peeled and julienned ripe peaches

**For the fritters:**

1 cup (8 ounces) whole-milk ricotta, cold

2 large eggs, lightly beaten

⅓ cup all-purpose flour, divided

1 tablespoon superfine granulated sugar

Pinch of kosher salt

2 ounces semisweet chocolate, melted, at room temperature

Canola oil, for deep-frying

Powdered sugar, in a shaker or small strainer

Prepare the peaches: In a mixing bowl, whisk together the honey and wine. Fold in the peaches, cover and refrigerate for a few hours.

Make the fritters: If the ricotta seems watery, place it in a strainer and let it drain for 1 hour, then return to the refrigerator to chill. Place the ricotta in a mixing bowl and whisk until creamy. Whisk in the eggs until completely incorporated. Whisk in one quarter of the flour until smooth, then add the remainder of the flour, one quarter at a time, until the batter is smooth. Whisk in the sugar and salt. Then, while whisking rapidly, add the melted chocolate. The chocolate will initially seize in the cold mixture, but as you whisk, it will speckle in the batter. Let rest at room temperature for about 1½ hours. The batter can be refrigerated for several hours, but it should sit at room temperature for 30 minutes before frying.

To fry: Heat 1½ inches of oil in a 3- to 4-quart saucepan until it reaches 350° on a candy or deep-fry thermometer. Using two spoons, shape about 1 tablespoon of the batter into a football (quenelle) shape and carefully lower it into the oil. When the bottom is a rich golden brown, turn the fritter over to brown the second side. Continue to turn the fritter to cook evenly, frying for a total of about 4 to 5 minutes. Transfer the fritter to a paper-towel-lined surface and let cool slightly. Break it open and check the inside. It should be cooked throughout. If the fritter is still runny in the center, lower the heat to reduce the oil temperature to 325°.

Continue to cook the fritters in batches and drain on paper towels. Do not overcrowd the pan. If the fritters cool down too much as you complete the frying, they can be redipped in the hot oil for a few seconds and drained just as you are ready to serve them.

Meanwhile, divide the peaches among bowls, spooning some of the syrup around the peaches. Scatter the fritters over and dust the top with powdered sugar.

# Brownie-Caramel Sandwiches

You can never go wrong with a pan of brownies, and these rich, chocolate-chunk brownies are made even better with a thin layer of rich caramel jam sandwiched between the layers. I like combining milk and dark chocolate for the chunks, but feel free to use any chocolate you like. Also: Make more brownies than you need, wrap them and freeze. You'll be glad you did.

*For the caramel jam:*

1 cup sugar

1 tablespoon light corn syrup

¼ cup plus 2 tablespoons heavy cream, hot

3 tablespoons unsalted butter, at room temperature

½ teaspoon pure vanilla extract

*For the brownies:*

Butter and flour, for the pan

3 large eggs

1½ cups sugar

12 tablespoons (1½ sticks) unsalted butter, melted, at room temperature

3 ounces unsweetened chocolate, melted, at room temperature

¾ cup all-purpose flour

½ teaspoon kosher salt

2 ounces milk chocolate, cut into chip-size chunks

2 ounces bittersweet chocolate, cut into chip-size chunks

*makes* **8 LARGE** *brownies*

Make the caramel jam: Put the sugar, corn syrup and 2 tablespoons of water in a heavy saucepan. Stir to combine and place over medium heat. Bring to a rapid simmer. Cook, swirling the pan from time to time, until the caramel becomes a deep amber color and wisps of steam rise from the surface. Remove from the heat; slowly stir in the cream (if the cream is added too quickly, it bubbles up too much). When the bubbling subsides and the sauce is smooth, stir in the butter and vanilla. Pour the mixture into a bowl to cool while you make the brownies.

Make the brownies: Preheat the oven to 350°. Butter an 8- to 9-inch square baking pan. Line the bottom with parchment paper, then butter and flour the parchment and the sides of the pan.

In the bowl of a stand mixer fitted with the paddle attachment, beat the eggs and sugar at medium-high speed until the mixture has thickened and is light yellow, about 3 minutes. Pour in the melted butter, then the melted chocolate, and mix until thoroughly combined. Mix in the flour and salt, then fold in the chocolate chunks. Pour the batter into the baking pan. Smooth the top, making sure that the batter reaches the corners of the pan. Bake for 35 to 40 minutes or until a cake tester or toothpick inserted in the center comes out with a few crumbs clinging to it. (Because there are chocolate chunks, test the brownies in more than one spot.) Cool the brownies in the pan for 15 minutes, then unmold and invert onto a baking sheet; let cool to room temperature.

Fill the brownies: The caramel jam should be firm enough to spread. If it's too stiff, microwave it for a few seconds. If it's too soft, refrigerate it to firm it up. Wrap the brownie block in plastic and refrigerate or place in the freezer until very cold (this will make it easier to cut the block).

Using a long knife, cut the block in half horizontally. Remove the top layer with a very wide spatula or, even better, a rimless baking sheet. Spread a ⅛-inch-thick layer of caramel jam over the bottom layer of the brownie. (You will have some extra caramel.) Carefully place the top layer of brownie over the caramel jam. Using the bottom of the baking sheet or the spatula, press down gently on the top to compress the brownie. Trim the sides. Cut the brownie into 4 squares, then cut each square on the diagonal to make 8 large triangular brownies. For smaller brownies, cut each triangle in half for a total of 16. Wrap the brownies individually in plastic wrap. Leave at room temperature for up to 1 day to firm up. For longer storage, refrigerate or freeze the brownies but return to room temperature before serving.

# White Chocolate Meyer Lemon Curd with Blueberries

White chocolate can't be classified as "chocolate" because it doesn't contain cocoa solids—only cocoa butter, sugar and milk solids. But I snuck it into this book because I love this recipe. Although white chocolate on its own can be overwhelmingly sweet, adding it to the base of lemon curd creates a richness and balance that's hard to describe. You'll just have to try it to see for yourself. Other berries can be substituted for the blueberries, and if Meyer lemons aren't available, just use another variety.

*For the curd (makes 2 cups):*

8 tablespoons (1 stick) unsalted butter

½ cup sugar

⅔ cup Meyer lemon juice

4 large eggs, lightly beaten

4 ounces white chocolate, finely chopped

*For the blueberries:*

2 tablespoons sugar

2 teaspoons Meyer lemon juice

3 cups blueberries

4 large mint leaves

serves 8

Make the curd: Place a double boiler over simmering water and add the butter. When it has melted, whisk in the sugar until the mixture is smooth and glossy. Whisk in the lemon juice and heat the mixture until it's warm and the sugar has dissolved. Whisk in the eggs and continue to cook the curd, whisking constantly, for about 4 minutes or until it has thickened and the whisk leaves a trail in the curd. (Don't be concerned if you see a few small bits of egg white in the mixture.)

Remove the pan from the heat and whisk in the white chocolate until it's melted. Strain the curd through a fine-mesh strainer. Spoon into serving bowls or glasses. Refrigerate for several hours to thicken.

Make the blueberries: In a small saucepan, bring the sugar and 2 tablespoons of water to a simmer, stirring to dissolve the sugar. Remove the pan from the heat and stir in the lemon juice. Place the blueberries in a large bowl, add the syrup and toss. Stack the mint leaves, roll them up and cut crosswise into thin ribbons. Toss the mint with the berries.

To serve, spoon the blueberry mixture over each serving of curd.

# Choosing Chocolate

With all the varieties and styles that are available, selecting chocolate may seem overwhelming. It's easy to understand that unsweetened chocolate and cocoa have no sugar, but it's harder to define semisweet and bittersweet chocolate. The terms are not regulated, so the percentage of cacao that's present in varieties described by those terms varies greatly.

In this book, I refer to semisweet chocolate as a chocolate that has between 62% and 66% cacao, and bittersweet as a chocolate that has between 70% and 74% cacao. The percentages refer to the amount of cocoa solids and cocoa butter in the product. The higher the number, the deeper the chocolate flavor and the lower the sugar content.

Regardless of the cacao percentage, the only way to select the right chocolate for you is to taste, taste and taste some more to find the brand and percentage that you like best. I most often find myself using chocolates made by Valrhona, Guittard and Scharffen Berger, but I love to experiment. It's worth seeking out brands that offer *feves*, or small baking disks, which eliminate the chopping that's necessary with big blocks of chocolate. You'll notice that I don't call for chocolate chips in these recipes, which is purely a matter of preference. I prefer my final creations to feature the irregular shape of chocolate that's been cut off a larger block. In the end, course, it's up to you.

# Frozen Milk Chocolate Parfait with Hazelnut Praline

Unwrapping Hershey's kisses and letting them slowly melt in my mouth is one of my earliest chocolate memories. This dessert reminds me how good milk chocolate can be. Now that I'm an adult, gianduja (a mixture of chocolate and hazelnut) is one of my favorite flavors, so I've added a crunchy hazelnut garnish. Parfaits are a little richer and creamier than frozen mousses. Parfait comes from the French word that means "perfect," and I couldn't agree more.

*For the hazelnut praline:*
Canola oil, for the baking sheet
1 cup sugar
½ cup light corn syrup
½ teaspoon kosher salt
1 cup hazelnuts, roasted, most of the skins rubbed off

*For the milk chocolate parfait:*
Melted butter, for the pan
12 large egg yolks
¼ cup sugar
2½ cups heavy cream, divided
¼ cup brewed espresso
1 teaspoon pure vanilla extract
1 pound milk chocolate, melted

serves 12

Make the praline: Generously oil a baking sheet. Combine the sugar, corn syrup, salt and ⅓ cup of water in a medium saucepan. Bring to a boil and cook until the syrup is amber colored and registers 350° on a candy thermometer, about 5 minutes. Remove the pan from the heat and stir in the hazelnuts with a spatula. Return to medium heat and stir to coat the hazelnuts in the syrup, then quickly spread the hot praline on the prepared baking sheet, being sure to spread the nuts to distribute them in the caramel. Let the praline cool completely until crisp, then break into pieces. Store in an airtight container at room temperature.

Make the parfait: Brush a 2-quart (about 10-by-5-by-2½-inches) loaf pan or terrine with melted butter and line the bottom and short sides with a strip of parchment paper, using enough parchment to extend up and over the short sides to serve as "handles" when you remove the frozen parfait.

In the bowl of a stand mixer fitted with the whisk attachment, beat the egg yolks and sugar together at medium-high speed until pale and thick, about 3 minutes.

Meanwhile, in a small saucepan, heat 1½ cups of the cream and the espresso to just below a simmer.

Reduce the speed of the mixer to low and gradually pour the cream-espresso mixture into the yolks to combine. Scrape down the bowl and add the vanilla and melted chocolate. Whisk to combine. Put the bowl in the refrigerator for 1 hour or until completely cooled.

Whip the remaining 1 cup of cream into soft peaks and fold into the chocolate mixture. Pour the parfait mixture into the mold and freeze for several hours or (preferably) overnight.

To serve, break the praline into irregular shapes. Use the parchment paper handles to lift the parfait from the dish; if it doesn't come out easily, dampen a towel with hot water and wipe it over the bottom and sides of the pan to loosen. Remove the parchment paper.

Cut the parfait into slices, place the slices on plates or in bowls and garnish each slice with shards of the praline.

# *Chocolate Risotto with Crème Anglaise*

I consider myself something of a risotto connoisseur. I've made hundreds of variations over the years, but only recently have I taken it to the sweet side. First, I tried using arborio rice (the grain that's typically called for in risotto) in a rice pudding recipe. I loved the results, and the recipe snowballed from there: Chocolate was a natural addition, and including the crème anglaise took it to the next level. This unexpected dessert is rich, so serve it in small portions. Should you find yourself with leftover crème anglaise, use it as a sauce on a simple cake, freeze it into ice cream or use it in place of eggs to coat bread for the best French toast of all time.

*For the crème anglaise:*

6 large egg yolks

⅔ cup sugar

1 cup whole milk

1 cup heavy cream

1 vanilla bean, split lengthwise

*For the risotto:*

2 tablespoons (¼ stick) unsalted butter

1 cup arborio rice

¼ cup dark rum (optional)

1 cup hot water

1 vanilla bean, split lengthwise

2 to 2½ cups whole milk, hot

8 ounces semisweet or bittersweet chocolate, chopped

Superfine sugar (optional)

Kosher salt

About ½ cup heavy cream

1 cup flaked coconut or sliced almonds, lightly toasted

Make the crème anglaise: In a medium mixing bowl, whisk the egg yolks and sugar until combined thoroughly.

Pour the milk and cream into a medium saucepan. With a paring knife, scrape the seeds from the vanilla bean and add them to the liquid, along with the pod. Place the pot over medium heat and bring to a boil. Meanwhile, prepare an ice bath. Set a bowl with at least a 1-quart capacity into the ice bath and position a fine-mesh strainer over the bowl.

When the liquid reaches a boil, slowly whisk it into the yolk mixture. Remove the vanilla bean pod, scrape it again with the paring knife and add any additional scrapings to the mixture. Return the mixture to the stovetop and cook over medium heat, stirring constantly with a silicone spatula, scraping the bottom and sides of the pan. Cook for about 3 minutes, until the custard has thickened enough to coat a spoon and steam begins to rise from the surface. Pour the anglaise through the strainer into the bowl set in the ice bath. Stir occasionally. Once the anglaise has cooled, refrigerate it in an airtight container for up to 2 days.

Make the risotto: Melt the butter in a medium saucepan over medium heat. Stir in the rice and coat it evenly with the butter; cook, stirring, for about 2 minutes, being careful not to color the rice. Add the rum and cook until it evaporates. Stirring constantly, add the hot water and vanilla bean and simmer until the water is almost evaporated.

While stirring, add the hot milk, ½ cup at a time; add more milk only once the previous measurement has been absorbed. Repeat until the rice is soft but still al dente and the risotto is creamy. (You may not use all of the milk.) Scrape the seeds from the vanilla bean into the risotto. Discard the pod or save it for another use.

Add the chocolate and stir until it's completely melted. Taste the risotto and add sugar, a little bit at a time, if you want to make it sweeter. Add salt to taste, and adjust the texture of the risotto by adding heavy cream. The risotto should be very creamy but still hold a gentle shape.

Spoon some warm risotto in the centers of soup bowls and pour cold crème anglaise around the risotto. Garnish each serving with a sprinkling of coconut or almonds. Serve immediately.

# Drinking Chocolate

Drinking chocolate is the much richer, decadent cousin of hot chocolate. The chocolate is the star here, so use the best you can find. If you plan on serving the drink with something sweet, like Chocolate Meringue Straws (page 23), you may not need to add any sweetener. Most of the time, I like adding small amounts of honey, and on occasion a pinch of cayenne or cinnamon. Serve the drinking chocolate in demitasse cups and imagine that you're in a Paris café.

½ cup heavy cream

6 ounces bittersweet chocolate, chopped

Fleur de sel

1½ cups whole milk

¼ teaspoon pure vanilla extract

Pinch of cayenne pepper (optional)

Pinch of ground cinnamon (optional)

Honey (optional)

Whipped cream (optional)

Shaved chocolate (optional)

*serves 8 to 10*

In a medium saucepan over low heat, stir the cream, chocolate and a pinch of fleur de sel together until the chocolate melts. Stir in the milk and cook until the mixture is hot. Add the vanilla, then the cayenne, cinnamon and/or honey to taste. If you like your drink frothy, use a hand blender or frother to whip it just before serving. Top with whipped cream and shaved chocolate or just sprinkle with a very small pinch of fleur de sel before serving.

# Chocolate Grand Marnier Liqueur

Chocolate liqueur was a fixture of my parents' bar when I was a kid. Although I don't remember the brand, I vividly remember a bottle that had actual nuggets of chocolate floating in the liquid. I doubt it was actually all that good, but that childhood memory has stuck with me, and I've spent years tinkering with a recipe for an excellent chocolate liqueur of my own.

It turns out that the best version is quite simple. All you need is a base spirit (neutral vodka here) and some other flavorings. I combine the flavors of chocolate and orange using cocoa and Grand Marnier. But if you prefer a flavor other than orange, substitute Frangelico (almond flavor) or dark rum for the Grand Marnier. You can combine the liqueur with vodka for a chocolate martini, but I usually serve the liqueur chilled at the end of a dinner. Float some whipped cream on top to make it even more decadent.

½ cup sugar

½ cup unsweetened cocoa powder

¾ cup vodka

½ cup Grand Marnier

In a medium saucepan, bring 2 cups of water to a boil. Add the sugar, whisking to dissolve. Sift in the cocoa and whisk to combine. Transfer the mixture to a spouted measuring cup and stir in the vodka and Grand Marnier. Pass through a fine-mesh strainer into a 1-quart bottle or jar and refrigerate for at least 3 days before using. The liqueur will keep for at least 1 month.

# *Thank You!*

---

My love and thanks:

To my mother and grandmother, who cooked every day and instilled the same passion in me.

To my family (especially my husband, Tom) and friends, who have been the best enthusiasts and critics of my creations over the years.

To John Scharffenberger and Robert Steinberg, who opened my eyes to all of the possibilities of working with chocolate.

And, most of all, my deepest gratitude to my "brother" Neil, who has been my supreme taste-tester, bottomless well of encouragement and continuous source of inspiration every step of the way.

—*Susie Heller*

Share your Short Stack cooking experiences with us
(or just keep in touch) via:

 #shortstackeds      facebook.com/shortstackeditions

 @shortstackeds      hello@shortstackeditions.com

# *Colophon*

---

This edition of Short Stack was printed by Circle Press in New York City on Mohawk Britehue Ultra Lava (interior) and Neenah Oxford White (cover) paper. The main text of the book is set in Futura and Jensen Pro, and the headlines are set in Lobster.

Sewn by: W. E

# *Available now at ShortStackEditions.com:*